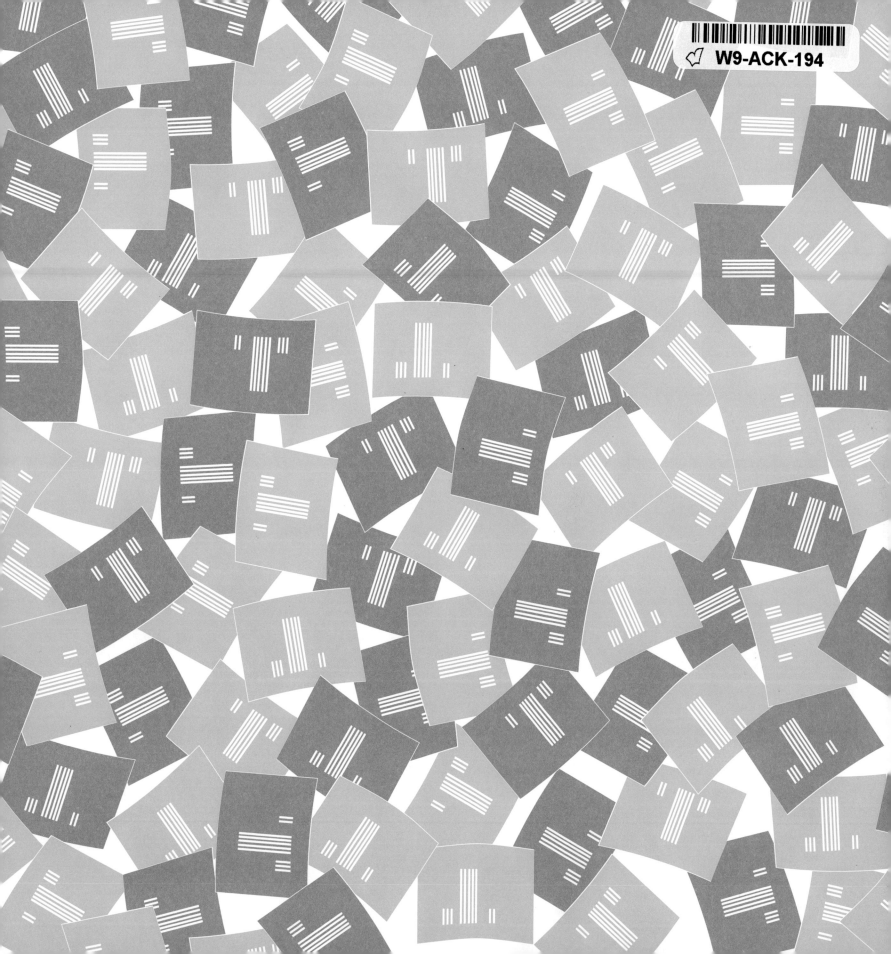

W9-ACK-194

Kids Talk About
Honesty

by Carrie Finn

illustrated by Amy Bailey Muehlenhardt

PICTURE WINDOW BOOKS
Minneapolis, Minnesota

Special thanks to our advisers for their expertise:

Dr. Kay Herting Wahl, Director of School Counseling
University of Minnesota

Susan Kesselring, M.A., Literacy Educator
Rosemount–Apple Valley–Eagan (Minnesota) School District

Editor: Christianne Jones

Designer: Joe Anderson

Page Production: Brandie Shoemaker

Editorial Director: Carol Jones

Creative Director: Keith Griffin

The illustrations in this book were created digitally.

Picture Window Books

5115 Excelsior Boulevard

Suite 232

Minneapolis, MN 55416

877-845-8392

www.picturewindowbooks.com

Printed in the United States of America.

Photo Credit: Library of Congress, page 30

Library of Congress Cataloging-in-Publication Data

Finn, Carrie.

Kids talk about honesty / by Carrie Finn ; illustrated by Amy Bailey Muehlenhardt.

p. cm. – (Kids talk jr.)

Includes bibliographical references and index.

ISBN-13: 978-1-4048-2317-4 (hardcover)

ISBN-10: 1-4048-2317-4 (hardcover)

1. Honesty—Juvenile literature. I. Muehlenhardt, Amy Bailey, 1974- ill. II. Title. III. Series.

BJ1533.H7F56 2007   2006003401

179'.9—dc22

Kids Talk Jr.

COUNSELOR: Sam

Hi, Friends!

My name is Sam Strong. I'm in the fifth grade at Eagle Elementary. I really like helping my friends with their problems. My friends call me "Super Sam the Problem Solver."

I've been getting a lot of letters from kids about honesty. When you are honest, you tell the truth. This is not always an easy thing to do. Read on for my advice about honesty.

Sincerely,

Sam

Dear Sam,

I told my friend that I could skate, but I can't.
What should I do?

Janissa

Kids Talk Jr.

COUNSELOR: Sam

Dear Janissa,

The best thing to do is to tell her the truth. She may help
you learn how to skate.

Sam

Dear Sam,

I told my grandma that I really liked the sweater she gave me for my birthday, but I don't like it. Should I tell her the truth?

Robin

Kids Talk Jr.

COUNSELOR: Sam

Dear Robin,

Sometimes we lie so that we don't hurt someone's feelings. You could give your grandma some ideas of what you would like instead of clothes. Even if you don't love the gift, be sure to say "thank you."

Sam

Dear Sam,

I told my mom that I did my homework, but I played on the computer instead. I didn't get my homework done. What should I do?

Tara

Kids Talk Jr.

COUNSELOR: Sam

Dear Tara,

You have to tell your mom the truth. Tell her that you are sorry you lied. From now on, it's homework first and computer second.

Sam

Dear Sam,

My dad always tells me not to lie, but he lied to me. He said that we weren't having pizza for dinner. Then he surprised me with pizza. I'm confused.

Greg

Kids Talk Jr.

COUNSELOR: Sam

Dear Greg,

This is what people call a white lie. Sometimes people aren't totally honest when they want to surprise someone. You shouldn't tell lies, but sometimes keeping a surprise is OK.

Sam

14

Dear Sam,

My friend stole some stickers from the store. She told her mom that I gave them to her. What should I do?

Gail

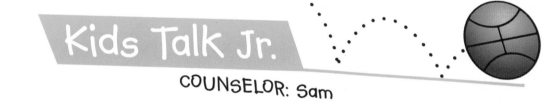

Kids Talk Jr.

COUNSELOR: Sam

Dear Gail,

Being honest can be hard, but telling someone else to be honest is even harder. Tell your friend that she lied and needs to tell her mom or dad what she did.

Sam

Dear Sam,

I really want to see a movie that my dad doesn't want me to see.
Should I watch it at my friend's house and not tell my dad?

Jared

Kids Talk Jr.

COUNSELOR: Sam

Dear Jared,

That doesn't sound like a very good idea. Your dad would be upset if you saw it. He trusts you to be honest. You should follow his rules.

Sam

Dear Sam,

I have a test this week. My friend asked if he could copy off of my answer sheet. Should I let him?

Celia

Kids Talk Jr.

COUNSELOR: Sam

Dear Celia,

Cheating is another way of being dishonest. It's not right for you to help your friend cheat. Let your friend know that he should study hard instead of cheating on the test.

Sam

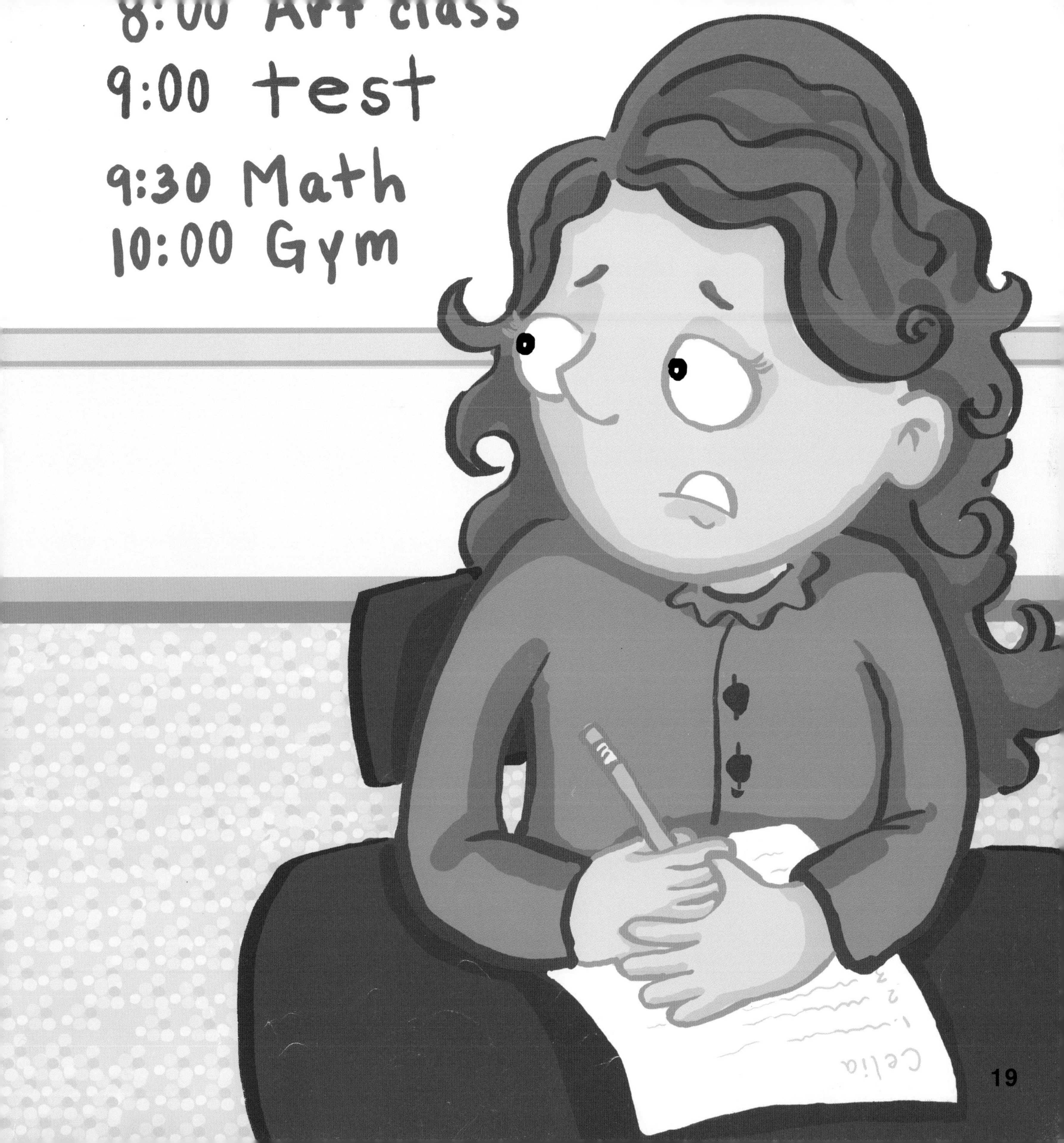
8:00 Art class
9:00 test
9:30 Math
10:00 Gym
Celia

Dear Sam,

I want a new baseball glove, but I don't have enough money. Should I take some money from my sister's piggy bank?

Andy

Kids Talk Jr.

COUNSELOR: Sam

Dear Andy,

It wouldn't be very honest if you took the money. Try saving your own money by doing jobs around the house or for your neighbors. The baseball glove will mean more if you work for the money.

Sam

Dear Sam,

The clerk at the store gave me too much change when I bought a juice. Should I give it back?

Charlie

Kids Talk Jr.

COUNSELOR: Sam

Dear Charlie,

You should return the money. You can show the clerk that you are an honest person. He probably made a mistake in counting. He will appreciate your honesty.

Sam

Dear Sam,

I made up a story about a boy in my class and told everyone. How can I take it back?

Larry

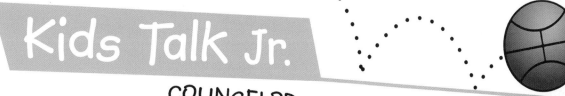

Kids Talk Jr.

COUNSELOR: Sam

Dear Larry,

You should talk to all the people who heard the story. Tell them that you weren't being honest. It might be hard, but it will make everyone feel better. You should also apologize.

Sam

Kids Talk Jr.

COUNSELOR: Sam

That's all the time I have for today. I'm off to the skate park to meet some friends. I hope I answered all of your questions about honesty. There's plenty more to read about. Remember, honesty is always the best policy.

Sincerely,

Sam

Grab a piece of paper and a pencil, and take this fun quiz. Good luck!

1. When you lie to your friend, you should
    a) tell your friend you are sorry that you lied.
    b) buy your friend flowers.
    c) keep telling lies.

2. If you are honest with your grandma about a gift you don't like, she will
    a) understand.
    b) buy you a new car.
    c) sing a silly song.

3. If you say you are going to study for a test, you should
    a) be honest and really study for the test.
    b) watch TV.
    c) draw pictures in your books.

4. A white lie is
    a) a lie that is the color white.
    b) a lie that smells like vanilla ice cream.
    c) a lie that someone tells when he or she wants to surprise someone.

5. The hardest thing about knowing that someone wasn't honest is
    a) telling the person to be honest.
    b) riding the person's bike.
    c) playing with the person's dog.

6. If your dad doesn't want you to watch a movie, you should
   a) make a movie of your own.
   b) not watch the movie.
   c) never watch a movie again.

7. Cheating is
   a) fun.
   b) not OK, even if you are helping your best friend.
   c) a good thing to do.

8. Saving money is better than
   a) taking it from your sister.
   b) drinking orange juice.
   c) learning how to count to 100.

9. If someone gives you extra change, you should
   a) hide it under a rock.
   b) keep it.
   c) return it.

10. Making up stories that aren't true can
    a) hurt the people the stories are about.
    b) get you more time at recess.
    c) help you make lunch.

ANSWER KEY:
1. a
2. a
3. a
4. c
5. a
6. b
7. b
8. a
9. c
10. a

Nellie Bly

Nellie Bly was a truthful journalist. She became the first woman to honestly report how women were being mistreated at the places where they worked.

Instead of just interviewing people and writing stories about them, she worked alongside of them. She put herself in their situation to find out what it was really like.

Nellie was very adventurous. She traveled to many different countries to report on wars. No matter where she was or what she did, she was always careful to honestly report what she saw and heard.

Nellie Bly will always be known as a daring, truthful, and honest reporter.

Glossary

advice—opinions about what should or should not be done about a problem

appreciate—to value someone or something

cheat—to fool someone or act dishonestly

dishonest—telling lies; the opposite of being honest

honesty—telling the truth

white lie—a small lie that isn't meant to hurt someone

To Learn More

AT THE LIBRARY

Guntly, Jenette Donovan. *I Can Tell the Truth*. Milwaukee: Gareth Stevens Pub., 2005.

Kyle, Kathryn. *Honesty*. Chanhassen, Minn.: Child's World, 2003.

Thoennes, Kristin Keller. *Honesty*. Mankato, Minn.: Capstone Press, 2005.

ON THE WEB

FactHound offers a safe, fun way to find Internet sites related to this book.

All of the sites on FactHound have been researched by our staff.

1. Visit *www.facthound.com*
2. Type in this special code for age-appropriate sites: 1404823174
3. Click on the FETCH IT button.

Your trusty FactHound will fetch the best sites for you!

Index

Look for all of the books in the Kids Talk Jr. series:

Kids Talk About Bravery	1-4048-2314-X
Kids Talk About Bullying	1-4048-2315-8
Kids Talk About Fairness	1-4048-2316-6
Kids Talk About Honesty	1-4048-2317-4
Kids Talk About Respect	1-4048-2318-2
Kids Talk About Sharing	1-4048-2319-0